WACO McLENNAN COU
1717 AUSTIN
WACO, TX 76.

Where in the World Can I...

SEE A VAMPIRE?

Where in the World Can I...

SEE A VAMPIRE?

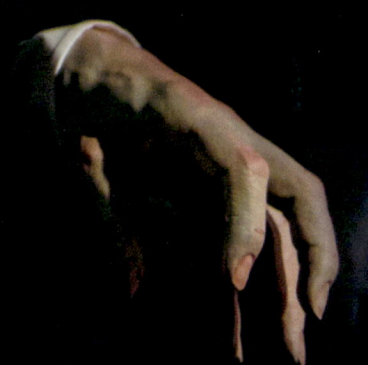

WORLD BOOK

www.worldbook.com

World Book, Inc.
180 North LaSalle Street, Suite 900
Chicago, Illinois 60601
USA

For information about other World Book publications, visit our website at **www.worldbook.com** or call **1-800-WORLDBK (967-5325).**

For information about sales to schools and libraries, call 1-800-975-3250 (United States), or 1-800-837-5365 (Canada).

© 2018 (print and e-book) by World Book, Inc. All rights reserved. No part of this publication may be reproduced, stored in a retrieval system, or transmitted in any form or by any means (electronic, mechanical, photocopying, recording, or otherwise) without written permission from World Book, Inc.

WORLD BOOK and the GLOBE DEVICE are registered trademarks or trademarks of World Book, Inc.

Library of Congress Cataloging-in-Publication Data for this volume has been applied for.

Where in the World Can I...
ISBN: 978-0-7166-2178-2 (set, hc.)

See a Vampire?
ISBN: 978-0-7166-2186-7 (hc.)

Also available as:
ISBN: 978-0-7166-2196-6 (e-book)

Printed in China by Shenzhen Wing King Tong Paper Products Co., Ltd., Shenzhen, Guangdong
1st printing July 2018

STAFF

Writer: Shawn Brennan

Executive Committee
President
  Jim O'Rourke

Vice President and Editor in Chief
  Paul A. Kobasa

Vice President, Finance
  Donald D. Keller

Vice President, Marketing
  Jean Lin

Vice President, International Sales
  Maksim Rutenberg

Vice President, Technology
  Jason Dole

Director, Human Resources
  Bev Ecker

Editorial
Director, New Print
  Tom Evans

Managing Editor, New Print
  Jeff De La Rosa

Senior Editor, New Print
  Shawn Brennan

Editor, New Print
  Grace Guibert

Librarian
  S. Thomas Richardson

Manager, Contracts & Compliance (Rights & Permissions)
  Loranne K. Shields

Manager, Indexing Services
  David Pofelski

Digital
Director, Digital Product Development
  Erika Meller

Manager, Digital Products
  Jonathan Wills

Graphics and Design
Senior Art Director
  Tom Evans

Coordinator, Design Development and Production
  Brenda Tropinski

Media Researcher
  Rosalia Bledsoe

Manufacturing/Production
Manufacturing Manager
  Anne Fritzinger

Proofreader
  Nathalie Strassheim

TABLE OF CONTENTS

- 6   What Is a Vampire?
- 14   Vampire Bat
- 26   Other "Vampire" Animals
  - Vampire Finch
  - Vampire Squid
  - Vampire Frog
- 44   Vampires All Around Us!
- 46   Books and Websites
- 47   Index
- 48   Acknowledgments

WHAT IS A VAMPIRE?

A vampire (*VAM pyr*) is a dead person who some people think comes to life at night to suck people's blood. Stories of such creatures come from many parts of the world. But most vampire tales come from Eastern European and Balkan countries, such as Albania, Greece, Hungary, and Romania.

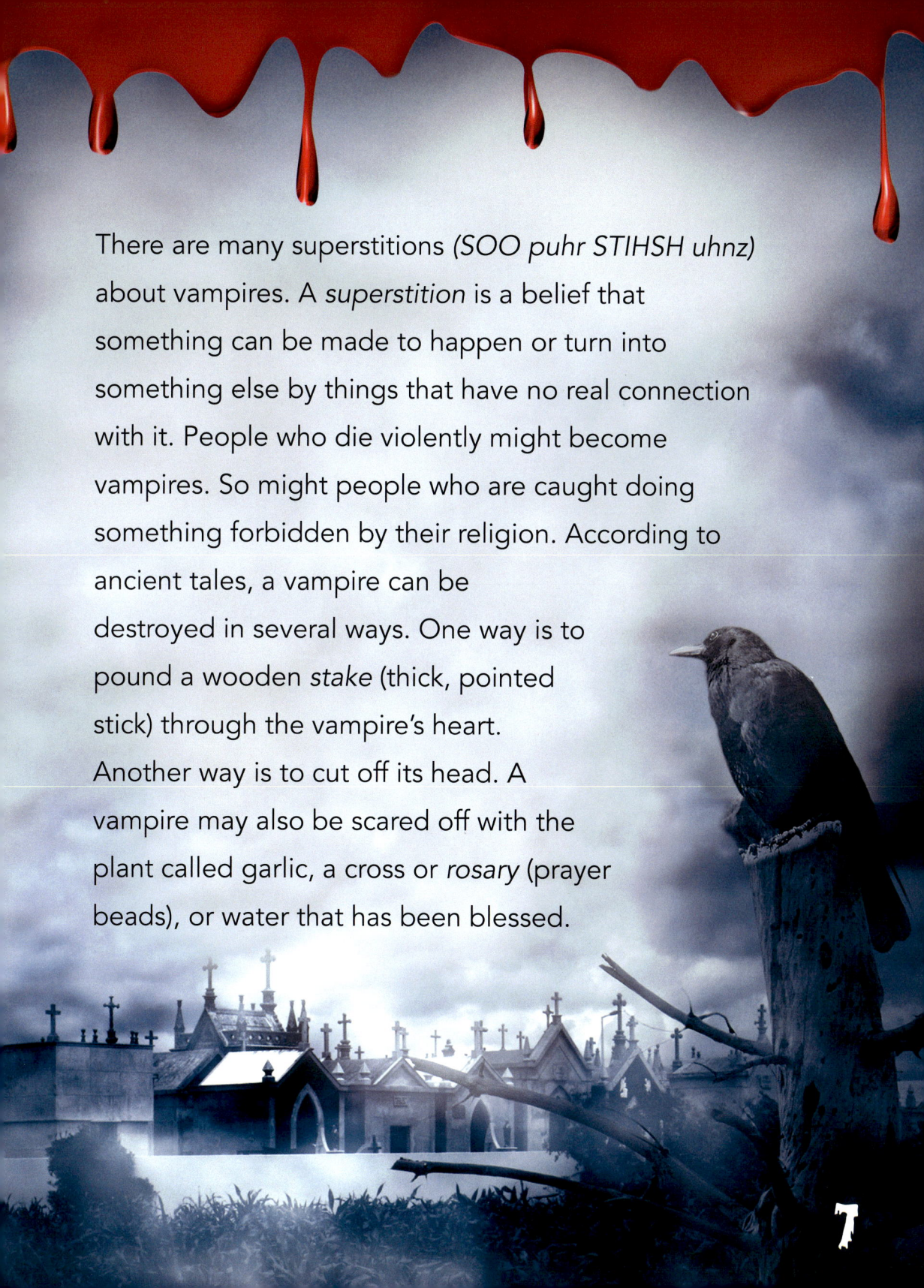

There are many superstitions *(SOO puhr STIHSH uhnz)* about vampires. A *superstition* is a belief that something can be made to happen or turn into something else by things that have no real connection with it. People who die violently might become vampires. So might people who are caught doing something forbidden by their religion. According to ancient tales, a vampire can be destroyed in several ways. One way is to pound a wooden *stake* (thick, pointed stick) through the vampire's heart. Another way is to cut off its head. A vampire may also be scared off with the plant called garlic, a cross or *rosary* (prayer beads), or water that has been blessed.

In Europe, from the late 1600's to the early 1800's, people dug up graves looking for vampires. In the early 1700's, Charles VI, the ruler of the Holy Roman Empire, paid scientists and doctors to search into vampire superstitions in regions of Hungary. These regions were captured in wars against the Ottoman Empire. The Holy Roman Empire included most of what are now the countries of Austria and Germany. The Ottoman Empire centered on what is now the nation of Turkey.

Vampire superstitions then spread throughout Western Europe. Christlob Mylius, the editor of a popular German science magazine, published an article on vampires in 1748.

The magazine came with a poem, titled "The Vampire," by the German poet Heinrich August Ossenfelder. This poem is probably the first piece of literature about a vampire.

In the written stories, a vampire is said to need a steady supply of blood to survive. Some stories tell about vampires biting the necks of sleeping people and sucking their blood. These people lose strength, die, and become vampires themselves. The horror story *Dracula* (1897) *(DRAK yuh luh)*, by the Irish author Bram Stoker, is the most famous vampire story.

The fictional character of Dracula is based on *legends* (old stories) of Vlad the Impaler *(ihm PAYL uhr)*. Vlad was a prince who lived in Walachia *(wah LAY kee uh)* (now part of Romania) in the 1400's. He was called "the Impaler" because of the way he punished his enemies. To *impale* is to push a long stake or pole with a pointed end through the length of a human body. But we do not know if these stories about Vlad are true. Vlad was nicknamed Dracula. In Romanian, Dracula means *son of the devil* or *son of a dragon*. Stoker used the name for his book.

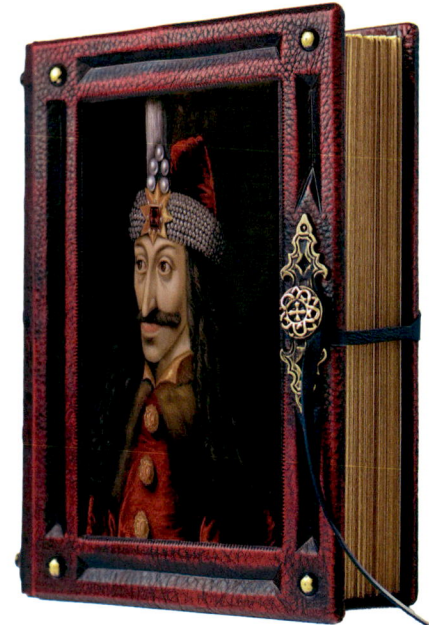

Many motion pictures have been based on Stoker's *Dracula*. The character first appeared in the 1922 silent German film *Nosferatu (NAWS fehr AH too)*. The Hungarian-born actor Bela Lugosi *(BEHL uh loo GOH see)* gained fame for playing the vampire in the 1931 horror movie *Dracula*. Books, films, and television shows about vampires are very popular today.

Vampires are not real, but some people believe in them. Many people have fun dressing as vampires on Halloween. But there are some real-life animal "vampires" in our trees, skies, caves, waters, and even in our own backyards! And you won't even need to carry a wooden stake to protect yourself if you meet one!

READ ON TO LEARN ABOUT THESE ANIMALS WHO ACT—OR LOOK— LIKE VAMPIRES!

VAMPIRE BAT

For a long time, people have thought bats might be *supernatural.* Supernatural means beyond what we know or understand. The vampire bat got its name because it likes to eat blood, just like the vampires of legend. A bat is the only mammal that can fly.

A *mammal* is a warm-blooded animal that feeds its babies mother's milk. Vampire bats feed on such warm-blooded animals as cattle, chickens, and horses.

Vampire bats live in Mexico, Central America, and South America. They sleep during the day in dark places. They hang upside down from the roofs of caves. Vampire bats usually gather in colonies of about 100 animals. But they sometimes live in groups of 1,000 or more.

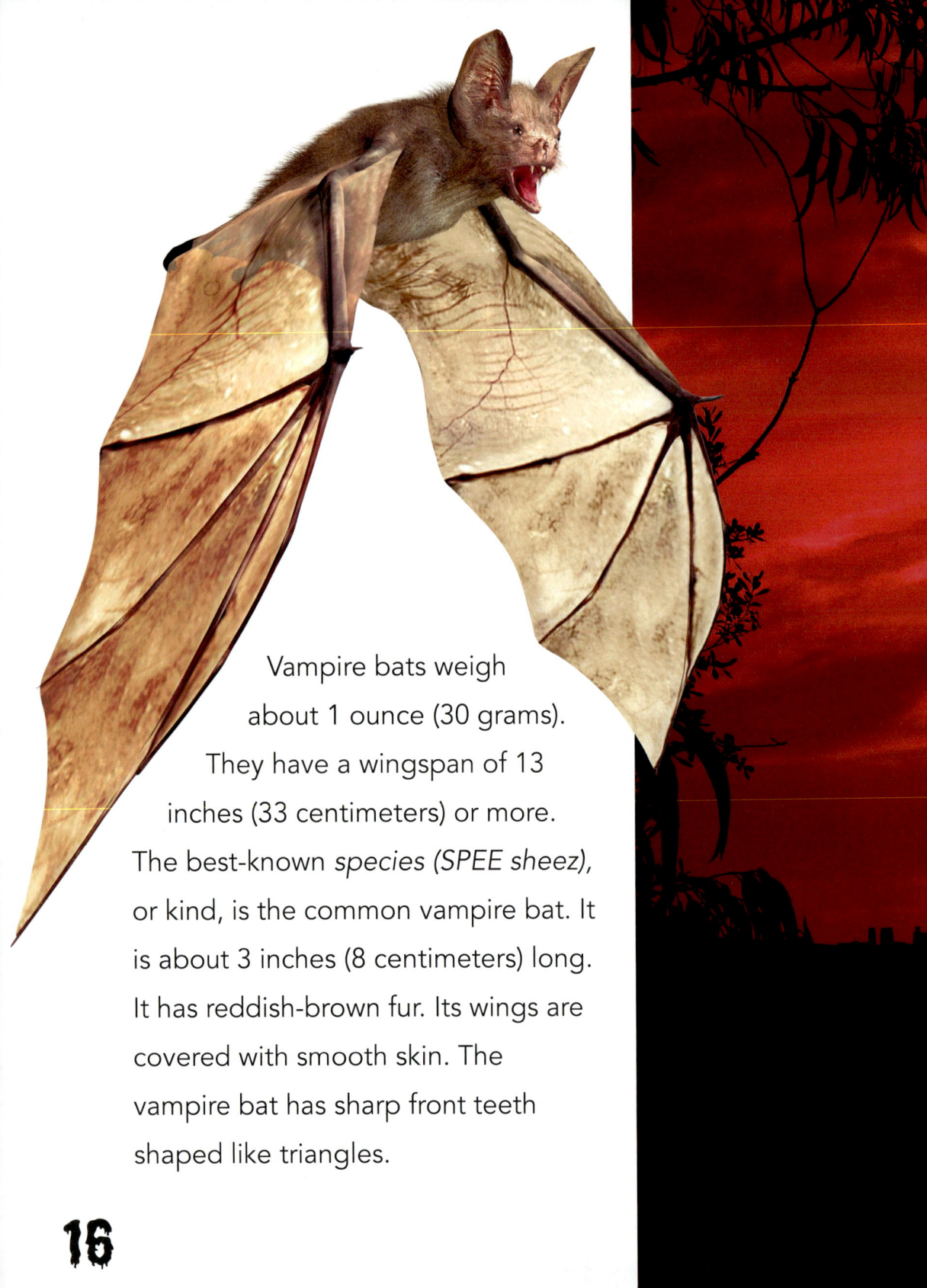

Vampire bats weigh about 1 ounce (30 grams). They have a wingspan of 13 inches (33 centimeters) or more. The best-known *species (SPEE sheez)*, or kind, is the common vampire bat. It is about 3 inches (8 centimeters) long. It has reddish-brown fur. Its wings are covered with smooth skin. The vampire bat has sharp front teeth shaped like triangles.

Like other bats, vampire bats have a special ability that they use to collect information about their surroundings. They make high-pitched sounds and listen for the echoes. The echoes enable the bats to locate nearby objects. This helps bats to fly at night in complete darkness. Some people believe that bats are blind, but this belief is false.

When a vampire bat is hungry, it listens for the breathing of a sleeping animal. Then, it sneaks up along the ground. The vampire bat pulls itself along with its powerful wings. It also has powerful back legs. Unlike other bats, the vampire bat can walk, run, and even jump!

The bat uses its nose to find a spot where the blood flows close to the surface. A vampire bat does not suck blood. It gently slices into the animal's skin with its razor-sharp teeth. It laps up the spilling blood with its tongue. Special chemicals in the bat's *saliva (suh LY vuh)* help to keep the blood from *clotting* (forming lumps) and keep the blood flowing. (Saliva is watery liquid in the mouth.) It takes 20-30 minutes for the bat to feed. During this time, the animal the bat is feeding on may not even wake up!

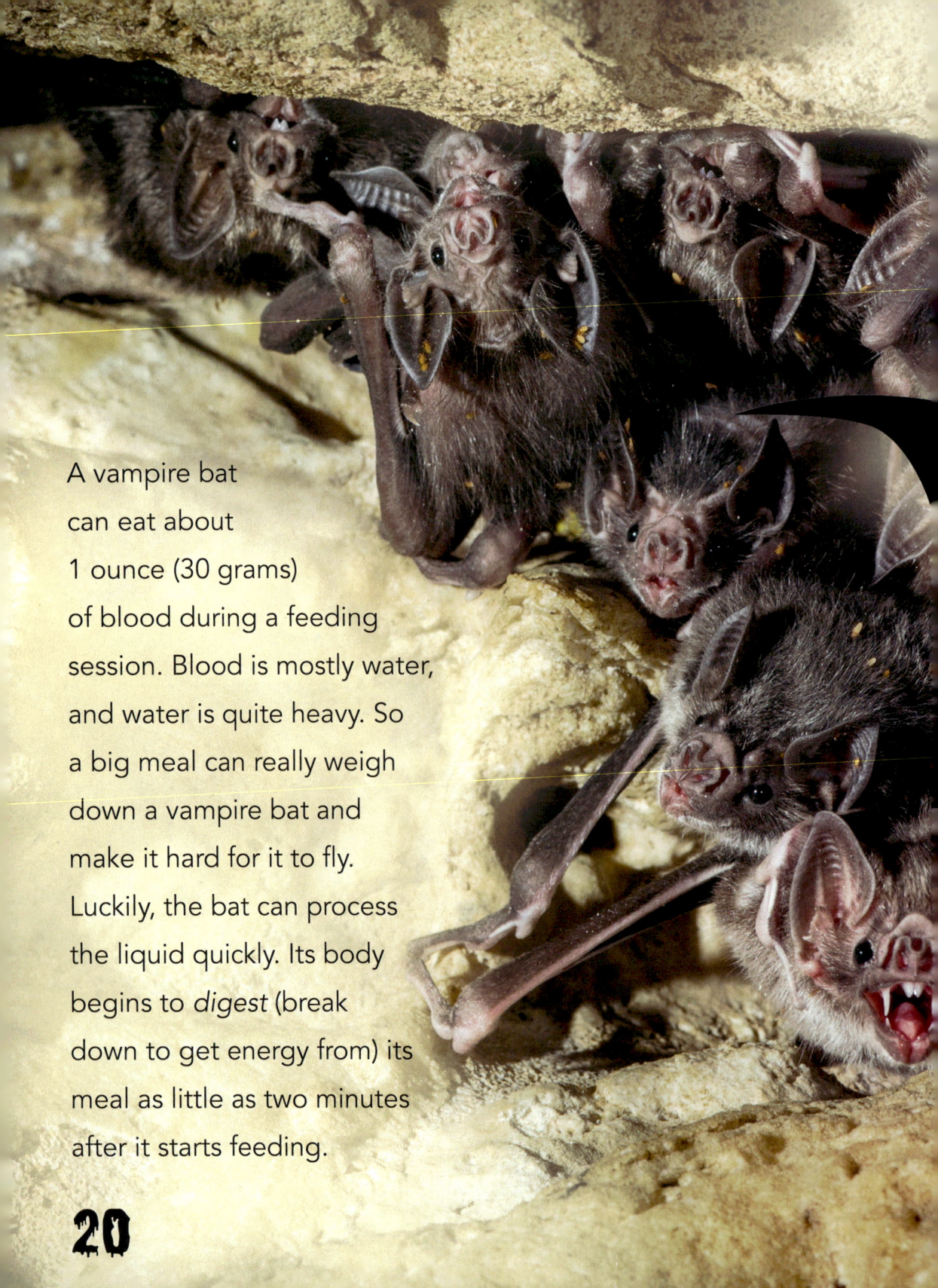

A vampire bat can eat about 1 ounce (30 grams) of blood during a feeding session. Blood is mostly water, and water is quite heavy. So a big meal can really weigh down a vampire bat and make it hard for it to fly. Luckily, the bat can process the liquid quickly. Its body begins to *digest* (break down to get energy from) its meal as little as two minutes after it starts feeding.

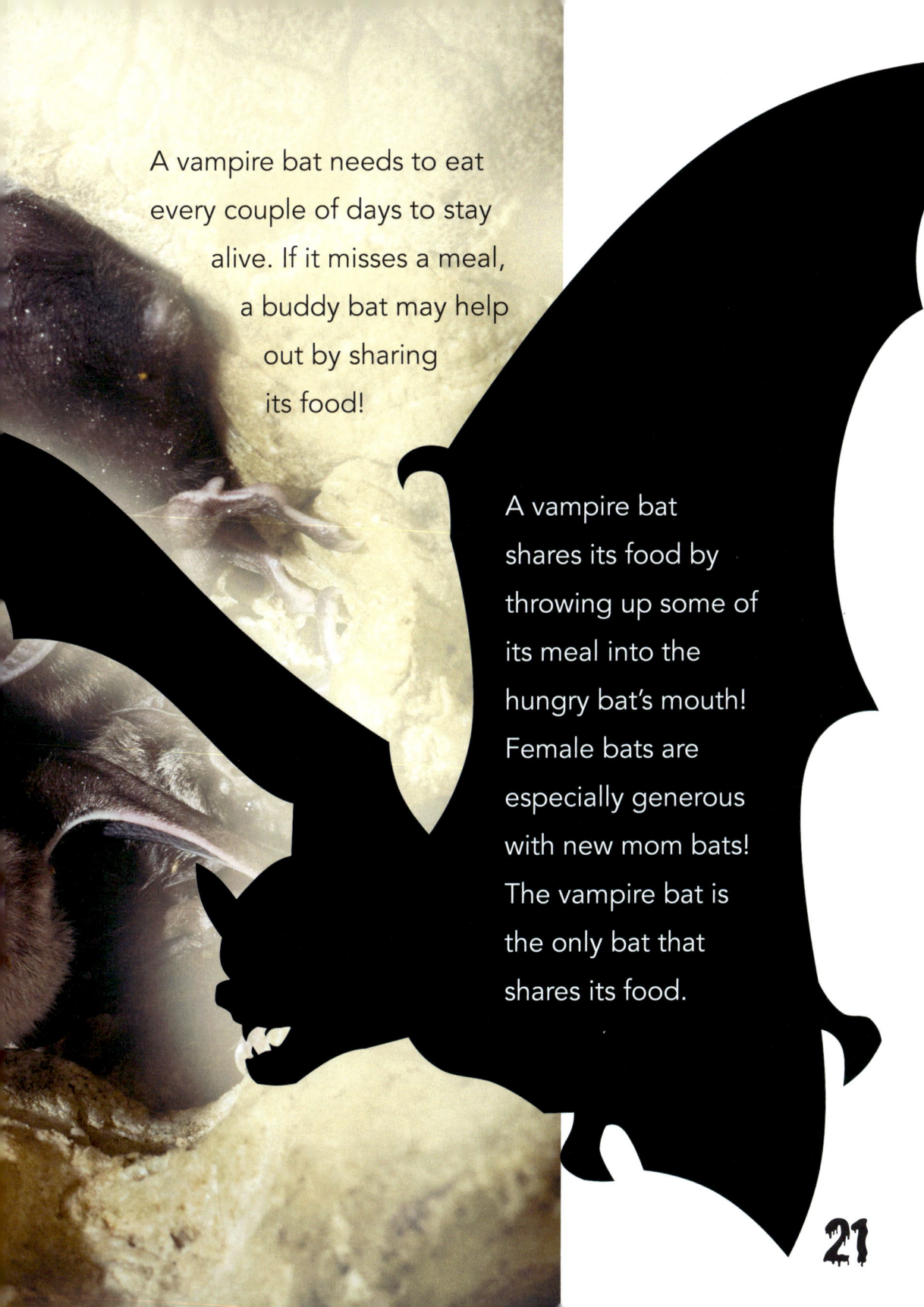

A vampire bat needs to eat every couple of days to stay alive. If it misses a meal, a buddy bat may help out by sharing its food!

A vampire bat shares its food by throwing up some of its meal into the hungry bat's mouth! Female bats are especially generous with new mom bats! The vampire bat is the only bat that shares its food.

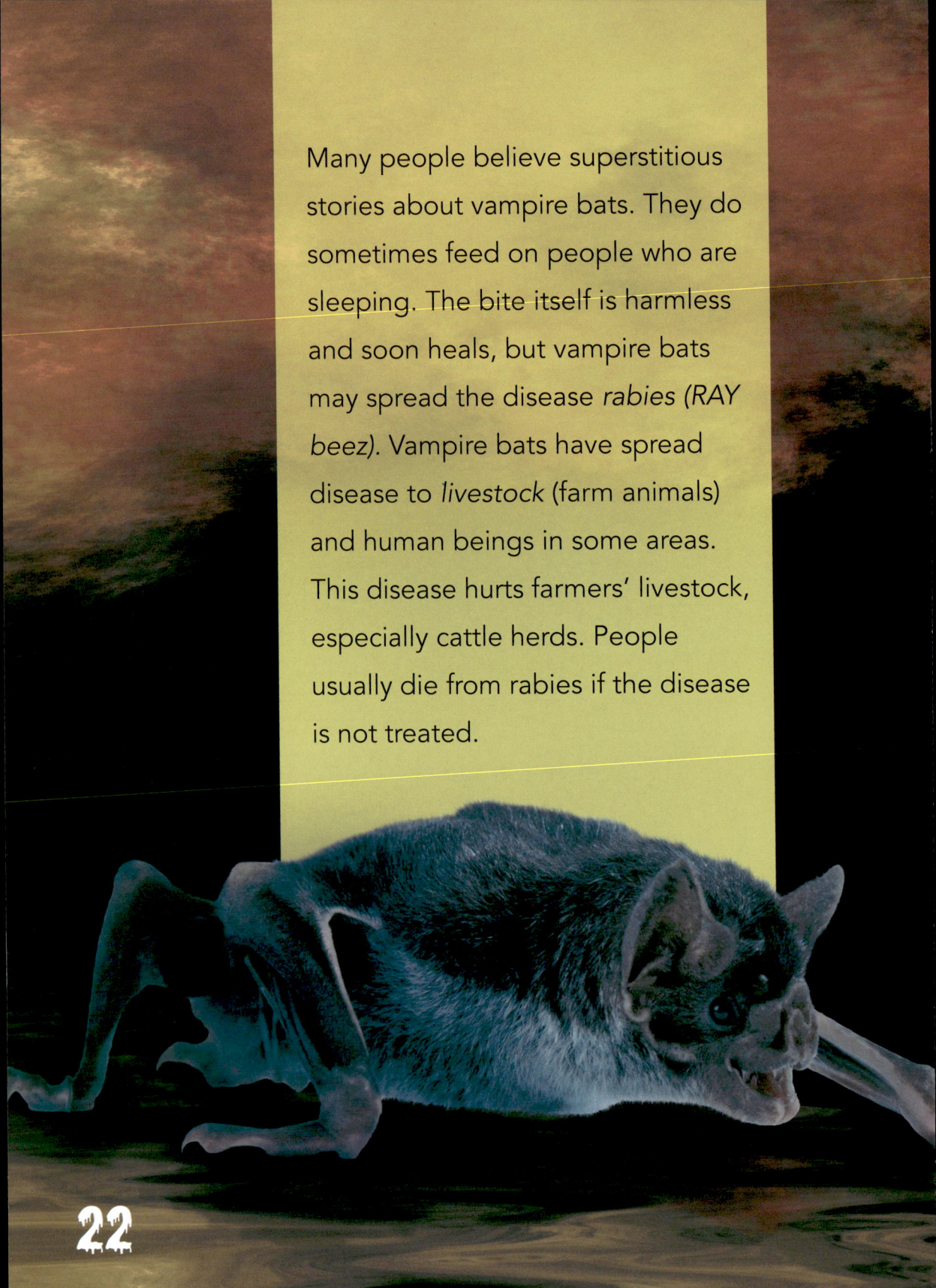

Many people believe superstitious stories about vampire bats. They do sometimes feed on people who are sleeping. The bite itself is harmless and soon heals, but vampire bats may spread the disease *rabies (RAY beez)*. Vampire bats have spread disease to *livestock* (farm animals) and human beings in some areas. This disease hurts farmers' livestock, especially cattle herds. People usually die from rabies if the disease is not treated.

But vampire bats are mostly harmless. In fact, the saliva from vampire bats may even help a patient who has had a *stroke*. A stroke is a sudden loss of activity in the brain. Most strokes happen when a clot blocks the flow of blood to the brain. The chemical in the bat's saliva that keeps blood from clotting may help thin a stroke patient's blood. This can help the patient's blood flow freely.

How can you see this vampire? You could go *spelunking (spih LUHNG kihng)*, or cave exploring, in Mexico, Central America, or South America. But this is a pretty dangerous hobby!

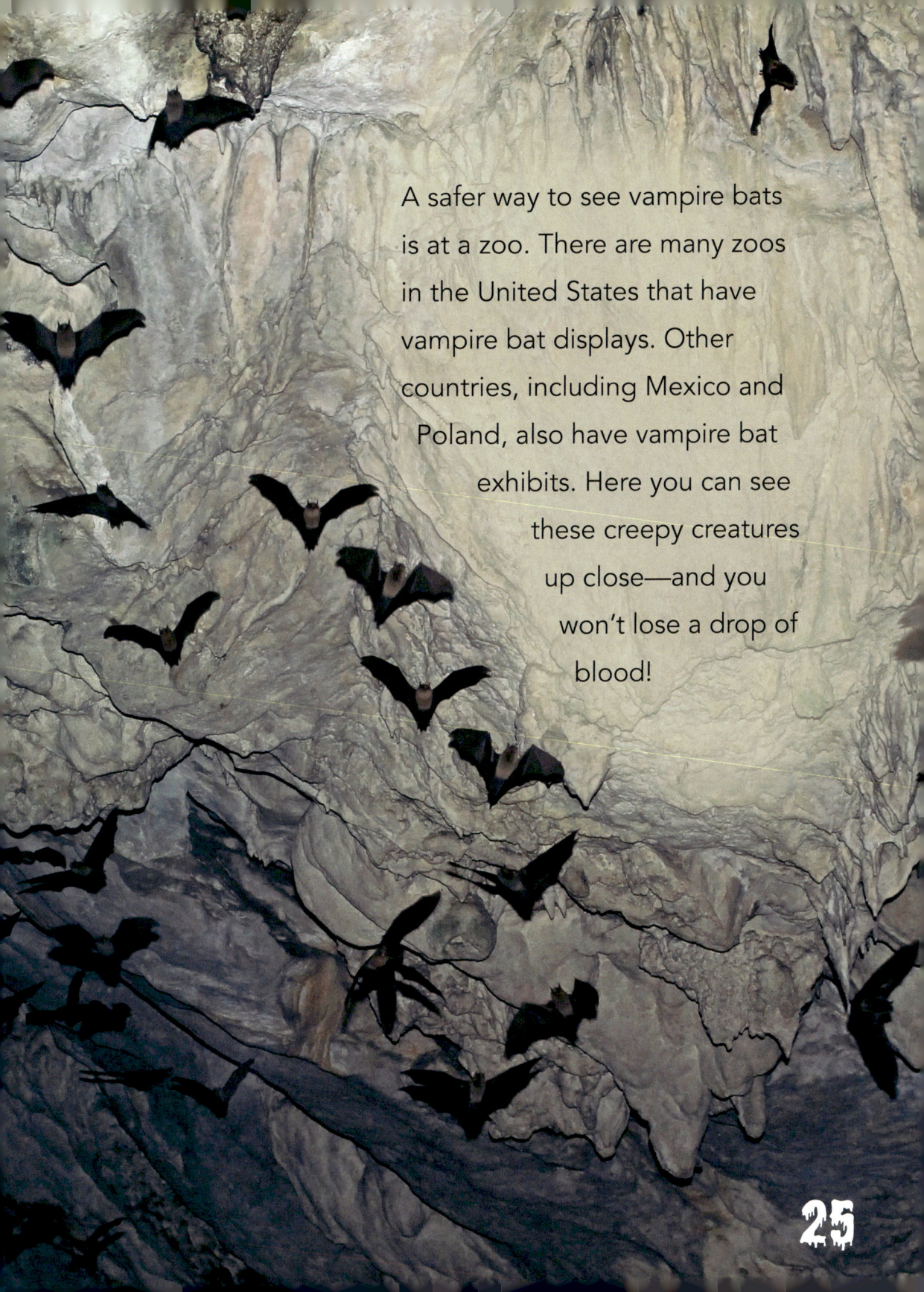

A safer way to see vampire bats is at a zoo. There are many zoos in the United States that have vampire bat displays. Other countries, including Mexico and Poland, also have vampire bat exhibits. Here you can see these creepy creatures up close—and you won't lose a drop of blood!

OTHER "VAMPIRE" ANIMALS

VAMPIRE FINCH

The vampire finch is another animal that got its name because it likes to suck blood! A finch is a small songbird. The vampire finch lives only on some islands in the Galapagos *(guh LAH puh gohs)* Island chain in the Pacific Ocean. The islands lie about 600 miles (1,000 kilometers) west of the country of Ecuador *(EHK wuh dawr)*. The Galapagos are made up of volcanic mountains.

The vampire finch is *endangered* because it is only found on these islands. Endangered animals are animals that could die out and be gone forever. In 1978, the United Nations Educational, Scientific and Cultural Organization (UNESCO) made the Galapagos Islands a World Heritage Site. Some of these places are special because of the plants and animals that live there. Others are special because of events in history that happened at them. Governments are required to preserve and protect World Heritage Sites.

The Galapagos became famous after the British *naturalist* Charles Darwin visited it in 1835. A naturalist is a person who studies animals and plants. Darwin wrote about the strange animals that live on the Galapagos Islands. His observations helped him form his *theory* (scientific ideas) of evolution *(ehv uh LOO shuhn)*. *Evolution* is the idea that living things developed over millions of years.

The Galapagos Islands have 13 species of finches not found anywhere else. This is more than on any continent. Darwin saw that the finches here developed as different species partially because they ate different foods. Their beaks developed over many years in special ways suited to the birds' different foods.

The vampire finch is closely related to other ground finches with pointy beaks found on Wolf and Darwin islands in the Galapagos group. As other finches developed beaks to handle many foods, such as seeds, fruits, or insects, the vampire finch developed its own special way of eating. When there are few seeds, fruits, or insects to eat, the vampire finch uses its sharp beak to peck at the feathers, feet, and skin of larger birds.

The vampire finch mainly feeds on the blood of the Nazca booby or the blue-footed booby. These are large seabirds found on the Galapagos Islands. The smaller bird pecks and drinks the *nutritious* (valuable as food) blood that flows from the wound.

The finch will also eat the booby's eggs. It will put its head on the ground facing down, lift its feet up, and push the eggs so that they roll off of a cliff and break!

Then the finch laps up the yolk. Other vampire finches will join in and help roll the eggs. They will also share in the egg or blood meal!

Boobies are the finch's usual target, but they will snack on almost any animal no matter its size. The animals that the vampire finch feeds upon are usually not harmed. In fact, they often do not seem to mind giving up a few drops of blood at all! Scientists think that the vampire finch developed a taste for blood from picking small parasites *(PAIR uh syts),* such as fleas or ticks, from the feathers and feet of larger birds. A *parasite* is a living thing that feeds off another living thing, called a *host*. The larger animals might think that the vampire finch is cleaning its body of pests. But it is really drinking blood—just like the fleas and ticks would!

VAMPIRE SQUID

The vampire squid is not really a vampire or a squid. It is more like a spooky, glowing, deep-sea monster! It lives at sea depths of about 2,000 to 6,500 feet (600 to 2,000 meters).

Its body is reddish to purplish-black. It also has webbing between its eight arms that make it look like it is wearing a cloak— just like Dracula himself!

The vampire squid is not a true squid. It is really an ancient relative of squids and octopuses.

It shares special qualities with both of these animals. The body of an adult vampire squid usually reaches about 5 inches (13 centimeters) long. The arms can extend another 10 inches (25 centimeters).

The vampire squid does not feed on blood. It has two thin threads that stick out from its tubelike body. It uses these threads to capture and eat "marine snow." This includes bits of decayed animals, animal droppings, and other animal waste and material that sinks down from waters above.

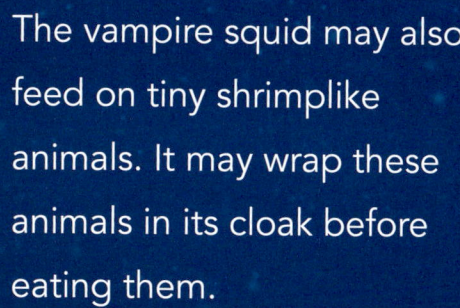

The vampire squid may also feed on tiny shrimplike animals. It may wrap these animals in its cloak before eating them.

The vampire squid uses fins on either side of its tubelike body to swim. It can also move by squeezing water to push it along quickly. The vampire squid can also turn itself inside-out! But it usually just floats without moving.

Little or no sunlight reaches the deep ocean where the vampire squid lives. But the creature can make its own light!

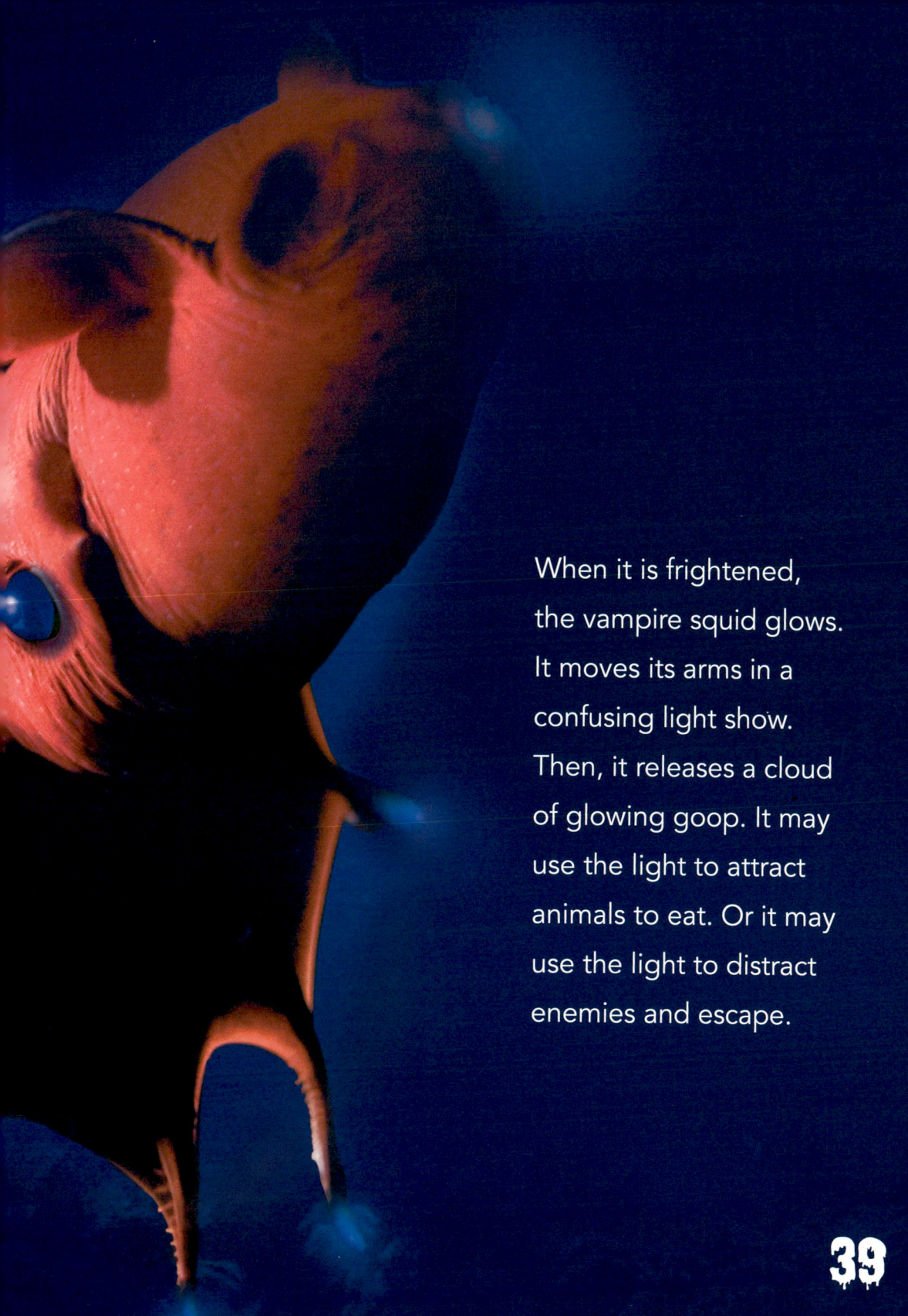

When it is frightened, the vampire squid glows. It moves its arms in a confusing light show. Then, it releases a cloud of glowing goop. It may use the light to attract animals to eat. Or it may use the light to distract enemies and escape.

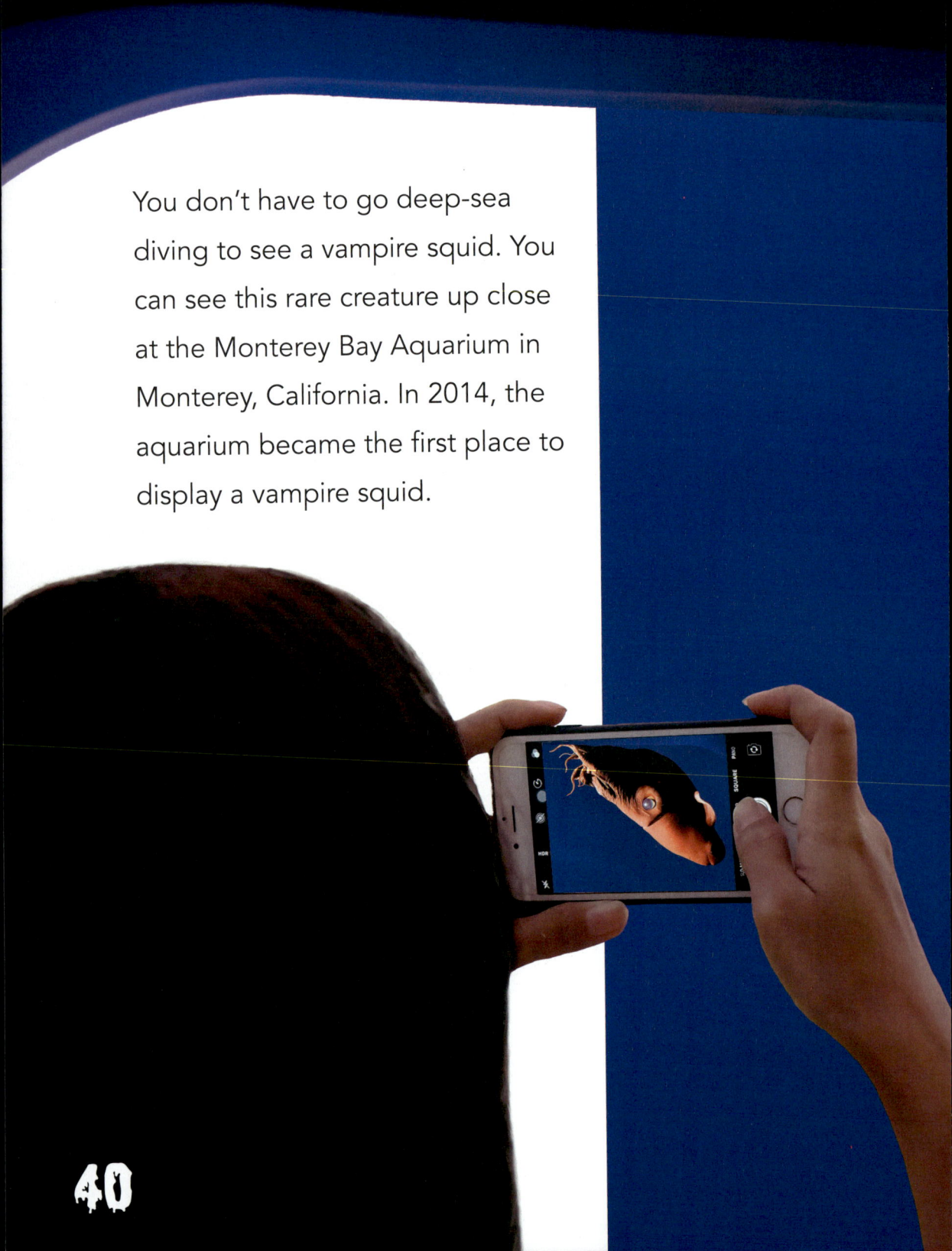

You don't have to go deep-sea diving to see a vampire squid. You can see this rare creature up close at the Monterey Bay Aquarium in Monterey, California. In 2014, the aquarium became the first place to display a vampire squid.

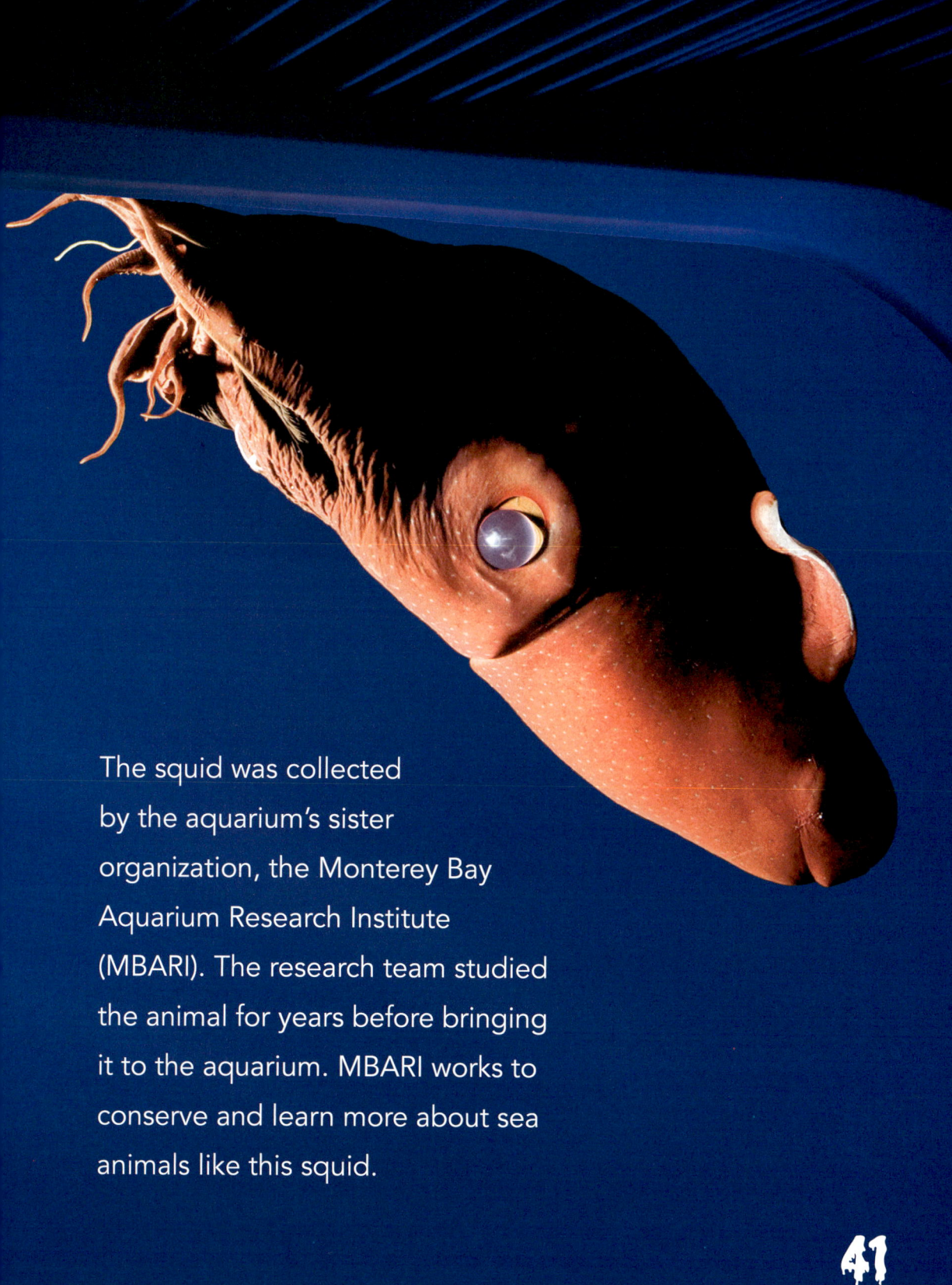

The squid was collected by the aquarium's sister organization, the Monterey Bay Aquarium Research Institute (MBARI). The research team studied the animal for years before bringing it to the aquarium. MBARI works to conserve and learn more about sea animals like this squid.

VAMPIRE FROG

The vampire frog is another animal that got its name for something other than its eating habits! This cute little frog looks nothing like a vampire! It grows to 1¾ inches (4.5 centimeters) long.

The vampire frog is also called the vampire flying frog. It uses its webbed fingers and toes to glide from tree to tree. The frog spends most of its life high up in trees.

This frog got its name because its tadpoles have sharp little black hooks in their mouth that look like fangs! Scientists aren't sure what the baby frogs use these fangs for. The tadpoles might use the fangs for hunting, eating, or gripping. The tadpoles grow up in small ponds in tree holes where the mother lays her eggs. As the tadpole grows up, the fangs fall out.

hooks look like fangs

This species was first identified in 2010. It is only found in the southern part of the country of Vietnam. The frog lives there in two protected areas in tropical forests.

VAMPIRES ALL AROUND US!

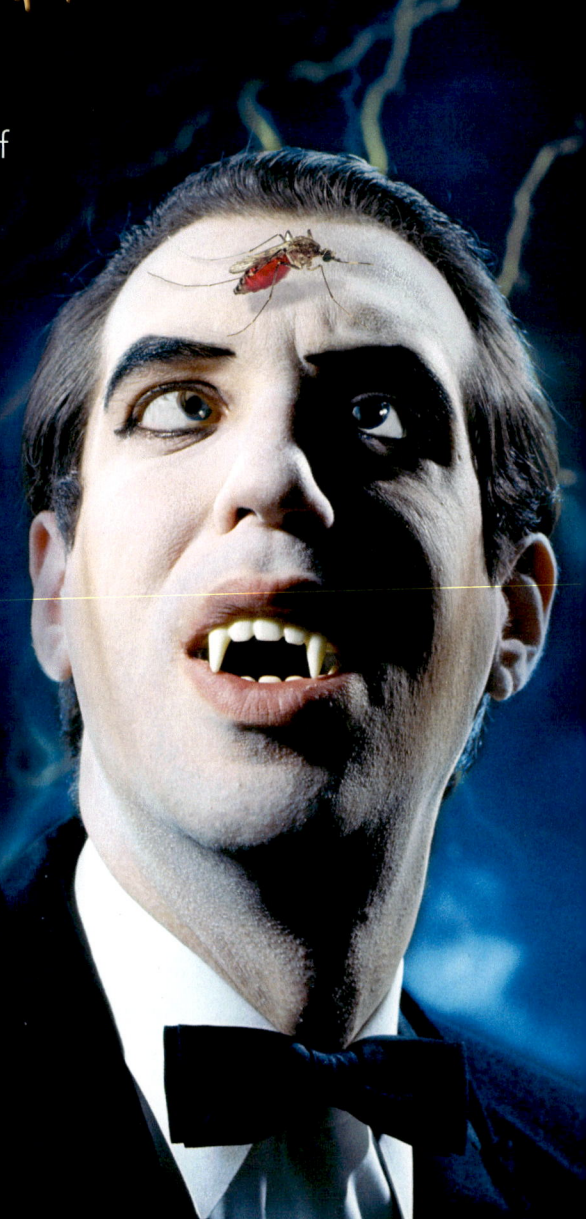

Unless you visit a zoo or aquarium, you may not be able to see some of the vampire animals you just read about. Others live in protected areas where you would be unlikely to see them.

But there are other "vampires" around us every day! They may be in our own backyard, on our pets, and even on us! These are ticks, fleas, and mosquitoes *(muh SKEE tohz)*! They feed on many animals—including human beings!

Ticks are tiny animals related to spiders and scorpions. The tick attaches itself to an animal and then pierces the animal's skin to feed on blood.

Fleas and mosquitoes are insects. Fleas poke into skin with their sharp mouth parts. Fleas grow to only about 1/8 inch (3 millimeters) long. But they can jump about 13 inches (33 centimeters)!

More than 3,000 kinds of mosquitoes live worldwide, even in the freezing Arctic! A mosquito's mouth has a tube that it uses to poke into the skin. Then it drinks the blood. Only female mosquitoes feed on blood. They drink blood to feed the eggs inside their bodies.

Vampires may not be real. But these vampire pests can be a real danger. Ticks, fleas, and mosquitoes can spread diseases in people and in animals. People can wear protective clothing and use insect repellents to avoid getting bitten by these pests. That's a lot easier than driving a stake through the heart!

BOOKS AND WEBSITES

BOOKS

Hanging with Bats: Ecobats, Vampires, and Movie Stars by Karen Taschek (University of New Mexico, 2008)
This book introduces children to bats from the animal kingdom to popular culture. Covers bat species, anatomy, behavioral patterns, habitats, and conservation, as well as a basic lesson on the theory of evolution and a survey of bats in literature and film. Also includes a project for building a bat house.

Vampires by Charlotte Guillain (Heinemann-Raintree, 2010)
This book introduces readers to what vampires are, how vampire stories differ across the globe, and where vampire stories come from.

Vampires by Dawn Martin (Hammond, 2009).
This book discusses early vampiric legends and a number of variations found around the world, as well as actual blood-sucking animals and modern vampires found in books, TV shows, and movies.

WEBSITES

Aquarium of the Pacific
http://www.aquariumofpacific.org/onlinelearningcenter/species/vampire_squid

A page from the aquarium with a species overview on the vampire squid.

National Geographic Kids
http://kids.nationalgeographic.com/animals/vampire-bat/#vampire-bat

Learn about the vampire bat on this website featuring photos, videos, and games.

Squid-World
http://www.squid-world.com/vampire-squid/

This website offers fascinating facts about the vampire squid and other squids.

INDEX

aquariums, 40–41, 44

bats, 14
  See also vampire bats
blood, drinking of
  by fleas, mosquitoes, and ticks, 44–45
  by vampire bats, 14, 19–22
  by vampire finches, 26, 30–31, 33
  by vampires, 6, 10
boobies, 30–33

Charles VI, 8

Darwin, Charles, 28
disease, 22
Dracula (book), 10–12
Dracula (film), 12–13

eggs, 32–33
endangered animals, 27
evolution, 28

finches, 26, 29–30
  See also vampire finches

fleas, 44–45
frogs. See vampire frogs

Galapagos Islands, 26–30

Holy Roman Empire, 8

Lugosi, Bela, 12

marine snow, 37
Monterey Bay Aquarium, 40–41
Research Institute (MBARI), 41
mosquitoes, 44–45
motion pictures, 12
Mylius, Christlob, 9

Nosferatu (film), 12

octopuses, 36
Ossenfelder, Heinrich August, 9
Ottoman Empire, 8

parasites, 33

rabies, 22

saliva, 19, 23
spelunking, 24
squids, 34, 36
  See also vampire squids
Stoker, Bram, 10–12
strokes, 23
supernatural, 14
superstitions, 7–9, 22

tadpoles, 43
ticks, 44–45

UNESCO, 27

vampire bats, 14–25
vampire finches, 26–33
vampire frogs, 42–43
vampire squids, 34–41
vampires, 6–13
Vlad the Impaler, 11

World Heritage Sites, 27

zoos, 25, 44

ACKNOWLEDGMENTS

Cover: © Aidar/Shutterstock; © Bob Orsillo, Shutterstock
2-7 © Shutterstock
8-9 © Denis Andricic, Shutterstock; © CTRd/iStockphoto
10-11 © Julien Behal, PA Images/Getty Images; Public Domain; © Shutterstock
12-13 © Shutterstock; Universal Pictures
14-15 © Eti Swinford, Dreamstime; Eric Kilby (licensed under CC BY-SA 2.0)
16-17 © Japatino/Getty Images; © Nathapol Kongseang, Shutterstock
18-19 © SuperStock/Alamy Images
20-21 © Nick Hawkins, Nature Picture Library; © Michel Mota Da Cruz, Dreamstime
22-23 © Netfalls Remy Musser, Shutterstock; © Jerry Young, Getty Images
24-25 © Shutterstock
26-27 © Michael Beder, Getty Images
28-29 © Varga Jones, iStockphoto; © Mark Jones Roving Tortoise Photos/Getty Images; © STILLFX/Shutterstock
30-31 © Jonathan R. Green, Dreamstime
32-33 © Shutterstock
34-35 © Steve Downeranth, Pantheon/SuperStock; © Creative Sunday/Shutterstock
36-37 © Steve Downeranth, Pantheon/SuperStock; © MagickStock/Shutterstock
38-39 © Steve Downeranth, Pantheon/SuperStock
40-41 © Mel Surdin, Dreamstime; © Steve Downeranth, Pantheon/SuperStock; © PIMPAN/Shutterstock
42-43 © Jodi Rowley, Australian Museum; © STILLFX/Shutterstock
44-45 © ClassicStock/Alamy Images; © Shutterstock